F U L L

a sensual evolution primer

FU
LL

a sensual evolution primer

by

NAKED THOUGHT

NAKED BOOKS

LOS ANGELES HOUSTON WASHINGTON DC
LONDON LAGOS

An Original Publication of NAKED BOOKS

NAKED BOOKS, a division of Thoughtdimension Inc.
Robertson, Beverly Hills, CA 90211

F U L L : a sensual evolution primer

ISBN: 978-1-105-67579-9

Printed in the United States of America

Edited by: Arletta Saafir

Cover Design by: Arletta Saafir

DEDICATION

This book is dedicated to my soul self that never allowed me to accept my chauvinistic program of hating my delicious femaleness. To my siblings Halimah, Munir, Ayesha, Latifah and Abi who witnessed my journey into fullness and empowerment, thank you for your constant stimulation, inspiration and love. I'd like to thank Ntozake Shange for unlocking the magic and liberation of poetry. To all my fellow free females this work is for you.

Contents

Acknowledgments 6
Preface 7
Introduction 8

FULL

Warrior Marks 11
Birth 13
Call Me A Bitch 15
Arletta UNVEILED 18
Dare Speak Me 20
Warning 22
MENSTURALGODDAMNMOONTIME FUCKINCRAMPPAIN 24
Unworthy of Love 26
Crazy Bitch 30
Scheme 32
Priceless Dick 34
Lies 36
XX Experience 40
Death 43
Psyche's Womb 45
Melted 47
Full 49
Unlovable Soliloquy 51
Emerging 53
Sexist Apocalypse 55
Kundalini Dreams 57
Evolving 59

ABOUT THE AUTHOR 60

ACKNOWLEDGMENTS

To all of my NAKED by Thoughtdimension MySpace blog subscribers for their love and feedback, and last but not least to my unfailing Spirit Guide A-UShoka for her flowing healing light through my words.

Preface

FULL is yet another gem released by poet Naked Thought that provokes, bleeds and inspires. In FULL, Naked Thought, with her trademark brutal honesty and heartwarming vulnerability shares her journey from womb hating victim to empowered pussy lover. Pulling no punches, Naked Thought reveals the steps of her evolution to self love and her reconnection with Goddess energy and her Divine Feminine. Her hope in writing this book is to inspire all women to embrace their wombs, earth mother love and creative sensuality becoming full as the force of nature each woman is destined to be.

INTRODUCTION

FULL is Naked Thought's poetry collection featuring her most intimate work. Gliding through what she calls the dark side of her past it shows her beginnings as an earnest little girl trying to find positive affirmation of the feminine being Muslim, Black and American and ends with her reveling in her immersion in the lush and full ripeness of sensual, empowered womanhood.

FU LL

"For much of the female half of the world, food is the first signal of our inferiority. It lets us know that our own families may consider female bodies to be less deserving, less needy, less valuable."

—GLORIA STEINEM

WARRIOR MARKS

I was ten
Womanhood emerging, bursting blossoming
Miraculous metamorphosis a magical springtime
Curves everywhere bomb ass legs, thick thighs, good and plenty ass
Aw shit when did all this get here?

I was ten
Skin couldn't keep up with lushness
Full roundness casualty of puberty
Stretch marks appeared Wondering Terrified awe
Witnessing girl to woman transformation

I was ten
Stretch marks were okay Didn't know enough to mind them
Until revealing glory to Mama she Disgusted
Afraid for my blatant femininity, burgeoning fertility
Searing heart ...brain with her comment
"I hope the man you marry don't mind them"

I was ten
Stretch marks emblazoned in shame
Hiding began pretty legs now grotesque
Each stripe branded with Mama's hatred of feminine
She transmitted diabolic shit

Thirty-six now
Warrior Marks Badge of Honor Sacred Wounding Trial by Fire
Warrior Marks Proudly claim every stripe
Warrior Marks Empowered beauty
Warrior Marks... mine

"Being born is like being kidnapped. And then sold into slavery."

—Andy Warhol

Birth

cloudy in my head spirit shielding
dead pockets where gremlins lie
absorbent energy hordes suck life dry
visions hazy obsessive using impulse guidance
who's blocking light of day
harmonic dissonance my daily bread
siphoning nightmares are corrupting dreams
amidst this nirvana visited me
pen sloshing through blue abyss
here where nothingness lurks truth is birthed

"I love to see a young girl go out and grab the world by its lapels. Life's a bitch. You got to go out and kick ass"

—Maya Angelou

CALL ME A BITCH

Go Ahead….

Call me a Bitch dammit
Brand me a Witch, Temptress, Evil Apparent
Delight in Female Reinvented
Spew the coveted compliments…
Ho, Cunt, Pussy, Jezebel, Woman

Thanks for acknowledging POWER of Feminine

Label me Illogical, Emotional, Indecisive
Refining misogyny Reversing negativity
Blasting centuries of debris
Encrusted lies in diamond shackles
Female conformity, Asleep with the enemy
Choice enslavement to status quo Eradicated

Yes… We take responsibility
For abetting oppression of pussy energy
Hip swaying defiance Annihilating
His-truth His-story His-religion His-world
This reality ceasing Initiating destruction sequence

Earth Mother scale balancing with
Her-story an EVOLUTION
(revolution in so yesterday and aint never worked anyway)…
Co-Creation of Our-World
Unleashed sensuality reigns supreme

Permission Granted
Go Ahead… Call Me a Bitch

When Ms. Parks decided she was worthy of a seat
Sat down to rest her weary feet
I guarantee the first thing that came to that bus drivers mind was
I know this black bitch didn't

Sister Harriet T went straight bitch mode when
Putting her pistol to shook negroes head and said
"There's no turning back"

Big Upps to all my Bad Bitches
Go ahead Call Me A Bitch

"Many spiritual teachers - in Buddhism, in Islam - have talked about first-hand experience of the world as an important part of the path to wisdom, to enlightenment."

—Bell Hooks

ARLETTA UNVEILED

Shadow self lurking
Lodged in space compression
Desperately Seeking Acceptance
Always power toning
Brilliance Restriction
Restrained beauty
All in the name of perverted humility
Some-bodies some-where informing
Men don't like powerful, feminine women
Repress true self, Will be misunderstood
Decided some-bodies where right, So I hid
Those some-bodies SCARED half-souls
Shook crowd pleasing *crooks*
Deliberate striptease
Layers unwound
Welcome to my world

ARLETTA unveiled

“Woman is not born: she is made. In the making, her humanity is destroyed. She becomes symbol of this, symbol of that: mother of the earth, slut of the universe; but she never becomes herself because it is forbidden for her to do so.”

— ANDREA DWORKIN

Dare Speak Me

Words don't roll off my tongue
Prefer being lodged in my throat
Tickle, Consciousness pricking Fear induced swallows of Constricted truth
Dare I speak/ What would the world say
Dare I speak/ What would the world think
Naked thought aint' exactly P.C.
Honesty usually isn't policy's best
Especially choosing irony outlined boundaries
Hypocritical VERBS metamorphosis
Stuck, Awaiting liberation
Dare I Speak Me???

"So it is naturally with the male and the female; the one is superior, the other inferior; the one governs, the other is governed; and the same rule must necessarily hold good with respect to all mankind"

– ARISTOTLE

WARNING (To the Overzealous but Well Meaning Muslim Men)!!!!

And if another crazy, fanatical, repressed, lustful
Wildly attracted to my enigmatic, irresistibly gorgeous ass , Masha-Allah
Muslim Man
Makes another comment of 'What I couldn't possibly know about Islam' or 'What I should do.'
My question is just "Who the fuck are you????"
Goddamn!!!!
I think I just might have to don a
Mothafuckin KIMAR and JILBAB and NIQAB
And try some Aisha radiallahanhu type shit and blow up they fuckin ass
(Islamic militant style of course)
I mean if you aint got shit nice to say then
Try following proper Islamic adab
And do as the beloved Prophet (SAW) would do and shut the fuck up
If you truly knew your Quran like you claim
There's no compulsion in religion. really is true
And you don't own my body, I DO!!!

"A period is just the beginning of a life-long sentence."

–CATHY CRIMMINS

MenstrualFirstBloodGoddamn MoontimeFuckinCrampPain

Fetal position, Envisioned annihilation
MenstrualFirstBloodGoddamnMoontimeFuckinCrampPain
Cursing each MENSUTRALFIRSTBLOOD drip
But MenstrualFirstBloodGoddamnMoontimeFuckinCrampPain Remained.
Devolving into a psychotic pussy abuser
Goddess eluded Moontime death wish.
She, Monthly mocking misogynistic intent
MoontimeGoddamn came like clockwork
MenstrualFirstBloodGoddamnMoontimeFuckinCrampPain
Each onslaught intensifying, Blinded to FirstBlood purification
XX HATE energy gathering momentum
Amidst rage CrampPain worsened
On the toilet for hours, callous flushing essences of female self
Twisting, my inside parts racked with hurt
Cursing My GoddamnMoontimeFuckinCrampPain
Became a self-proclaimed IBRUPROFEN junkie
Fruitlessly seeking quick-fixes from
MenstrualFirstBloodGoddamnMoontimeFuckinCrampPain
Downing 8-10 of those gorgeous brown babies
Each pill taunting in my self-loathing haze
False promises of oblivion from
MenstrualFirstBloodGoddamnMoontimeFuckinCrampPain
Self-destructive spiral festered ugly red shit
Forsook beloved MOON
The Almighty She denied me escape
Into illusions of male supremacy
Crying ...Ya Allah, Why did you make me a fuckin female!!!!
Asking answerless questions Clueless that
My MenstrualFirstBloodGoddamnMoontimeFuckinCrampPain
More priceless than gold. If my FIRSTBLOOD
Was anticipated, celebrated. Instead of shamefully ignored
I would have LOVED my pussy, affirmed in her awesomeness
MenstrualFirstBloodGoddamnMoontimeFuckinCrampPain
Thanked Mother Spirit. Blessing its magic, Transforming into
MenstrualFirstBloodMoontimeEmpoweringSacredPurication

"Women's apparent endorsement of male supremacy is ... a pathetic striving for self- respect, self-justification, and self-pardon. After fifteen hundred years of subjection to men, Western woman finds it almost unbearable to face the fact that she has been hoodwinked and enslaved by her inferiors—that the master is lesser than the slave."

–ELIZABETH GOULD DAVIS

Unworthy of Love

A Vignette Pt. 1
Naked Thought's Psyche
Impossible that he really likes ME
Was told too brash ,too bold, too ambitions, too soft,
too weak, too stubborn, to be husband material
Bowed, Tearless, Stoic Acceptance
Cauz I'm a soldier...Never let them see you cry...remember
Flawed, Must be true From then on knew
I AM NOT WORTHY OF BEING LOVED, I AM NOT WORTHY OF BEING LOVED
I AM NOT WORTHY OF BEING LOVED, I AM NOT WORTHY OF BEING LOVED
Innocent logic Never will be a husband for me
She...the 7 year old RULES ME
Confused medley of
Father GOD = Father DAD = Father HE
Pleasing God, Ya Allah = Pleasing Dad, So they will still love me
Approval obsession Seeking **God's/Dad's/His**
Our Father which art in Heaven, Ima do right, Secure my heaven space don't want to burn...
Please **Daddy, God, He**...Have mercy on me....
Fearing the Wrath of this God of Love and Mercy

Ar-Rahman (The Beneficent), Ar-Raheem (The Merciful)
This salve poured over my worries...no comfort...can't sleep... up late night sad and scared...ashamed I didn't make all of my five prayers today... frantically counting did I do more good deeds than bad need to do some more Sunnah prayers earn extra blessings just in case... too sleepy...maybe I can make up prayers tomorrow...yawn...this burden sometimes I hate it and hate Him ...no, I dare not think that... hell bound...don't want to burn...don't want to burn...restless sleep come... awake unhappy... convinced I am a bad, bad girl and Allah's mad at me and Dad doesn't love me...

HE's were greedy, Always **wanting judging demanding**
Obligingly obedient but Allah is never Happy with me
I AM NOT WORTHY OF BEING LOVED, I AM NOT WORTHY OF BEING LOVED
I AM NOT WORTHY OF BEING LOVED, I AM NOT WORTHY OF BEING LOVED
Couldn't find the Divine Love promised
WHERE IS THE MOTHA FUCKIN LOVE??? In this belief
Fear-grounded, Allah's Wrath, Hell and
Pleasing all of the He'S...Felt more like hating Him

...Feeling bad all of time... consumed with guilt...need to read some more Quran... be more like Prophet Muhammad...can't just be myself and be happy and say what I think...Allah is already mad at me...no matter how hard I try to please...oh well I AM a Bad, Bad Girl and going straight to Hell

I AM NOT WORTHY OF BEING LOVED, I AM NOT WORTHY OF BEING LOVED
I AM NOT WORTHY OF BEING LOVED, I AM NOT WORTHY OF BEING LOVED

...Honestly thought Hell was a stupid idea anyway and a God having nothing better to do than count and keep track of all of our sins is dumb and boring...I figured surely God has better things to do...I think...but I'm not supposed to think those thoughts...and so ...yet another bad deed on my record...oh well, after all not matter how hard I try I am a Bad, Bad Girl...going straight to hell...

All of these He's- **Allah, My Father, My Husband**
Fused in my psyche...
obey my parents, especially my Dad, is to please God
please my husband is to please God

...Pleasing all these He's made me tired,,, a thankless task I am never good enough anyway...but I so want to be a good girl...I am still a Bad Bad Girl

I AM UNWORTHY OF LOVE, I AM UNWORTHY OF LOVE
I AM UNWORTHY OF LOVE, I AM UNWORTHY OF LOVE

Please Love, Accept Me Don't Reject Me

Allah, Daddy, My Husband
Men, He's

...It was never enough, I can never do enough...I must please all of them, can't ris...k upsetting them, can't be truthful, can't be myself, I Fear He/ I Fear Him/ I Fear all of Them...And in my fear I hate my need of them...I Hate Them

I AM UNWORTHY OF LOVE

"Women cannot complain about men anymore until they start getting better taste in them."

—BILL MAHER

Crazy Bitch

Ever had a wonderful man treat you perfectly, Resenting him
Cherished you like the Queen you claim to be yet you responded angry
Massaged your feet while LISTENING open-heartedly
When moving in to kiss you, Perfect. Reverent insistent
Exploring contours of face lips. Sweet.
Paying homage to Divinity exactly how you like it.
Pushing away, telling him "no you didn't want to go there...today."
Saying "o.k., to trust him." Deciding to stay just to prove him wrong.
True to his word, over and over again.
Spent hours body worshiping
Your pleasure the only intent. Delighting in every curve
Discovering ALL of Your spots.
Every time you came up for air tasting yourself on his lips.
Drowning you in compliments,
Said everything you never believed always wanted to hear.
Read your heart secrets. Never felt loved like this.
Let you in, sharing dreams. Held you and between
the licking and sucking TALKED. Revealing himself
You wanting to scream "Why are you being so nice to me?"
In the midst of dream kind intimacy Rejecting
Kept his word, never tried to fuck
Showered you with love induced lust. Discomfited yet satisfied.
His rightness a violation somehow
Morning after a perfect night, left running scared.
Still desiring the other man, who ignores you
Preferring shit treatment.
Well, that was me and I need help.
Realized that I too was one of them
Crazy Bitchez

"On the day when it will be possible for woman to love not in her weakness but in strength, not to escape herself but to find herself, not to abase herself but to assert herself -- on that day love will become for her, as for man, a source of life..."

—SIMONE DE BEAUVOIR

Schemes

DIABOLICAL schemes/ by MEN/feasting off/ insecuritles/ earth rage/ of wet dreams/ DREAMS/ long forsaken/ in this/ senseless/ romantic/ WASTELAND/ wasteland of/ illusion/ LOVE/ love/ illusion/ love/ what is/ THIS LOVE/ is it/ fo' real/ can u/feel/ WRONG/ be wrong/ sell yo' soul/ for love/ for ILLUSION/ for strength/ strength/ that I have/ STRENGTH/ that u have/ that we/ IGNORE/ do not trust/ and are thus/ CURSED/ to wander through NIGHTMARES/ where/ the endless night/rented/ with SCREAMS/ of desertion/ no comfort for/ dry dreams/ who die/MOCKING us/ with gleeful eyes/ forsaking OURSELVES/ for menselves/ why would I give/MY ALL/ with no guarantee that u will SATISFY MY SOUL/ love watching me grow old/ and grow IN LOVE/ cauz if not/ then u aint worth/ SHIT of/ we time/ precious/ PRICELESS TIME/ so passion is SADISTIC JOKES/ made so that we/GLADLY/ madly rush HEADLONG/ enslaving ourselves/ to MENSELVES/ who only dwell/ in their own INSECURITIES/wanting no share of our INNER MANSIONS/ only our lips and/ our HIPS/ never OUR EYES/ accusing/ betraying OUR CRIES/ do menselves hear SHEselves? / so we shut the window to OUR SOULS/ that he MAY STAY always

"She even had a kind of special position among men: she was an exception, she fitted none of the categories they commonly used when talking about girls; she wasn't a cock-teaser, a cold fish, an easy lay or a sneaky bitch; she was an honorary person. She had grown to share their contempt for most women."

—Simone de Beauvoir

Priceless Dick

Amazing how we mimic our oppressors
Becoming exaggerated caricatures
ie. Female hating bitches
Rollin with the best of sexists
Sistas selling each other out for
Some of that *PRICELESS DICK*

"In civilized societies today ... clitoris envy, or womb envy, takes subtle forms. Man's constant need to disparage woman, to humble her, to deny her equal rights, and to belittle her achievements—all are expressions of his innate envy and fear.

–Elizabeth Gould Davis

LIES

Dwelled behind the veil for 31 years
I champion Muslimah
Imam Mohammed worshiper
Jihadist for Truth choosing
Shuttered eyes, willful blindness, feminine despised
Me...diminished blow by mothafuckin' blow
Each time I read the Quran
"Women are devoutly obedient (to their husbands)"
"Beat them lightly"
"Their courses are a hurt and a pollution"
"2 female witnesses for every man so she may remind her if she forgets"
"Marry 2, 3, 4 of them (always forgetting that)"
"But one is best if ye but knew"
"They (men) have a degree over you"
Female ego shattered
Crushed...broken heart bits stinging
Bitter antiseptic of blind faith
Male superiority prevails
Dismissing these verses focusing on
"Created humankind from a single soul and from it male and female"
"Male and female are equal in the sight of Allah"
No picking or choosing, True believers accept it all
"Verily Allah speaks the truth"
Pesky knots of irritation
Questions to persistent to be ignored
Eyelids dense...burdened with tears deferred
Consumed by patriarchy
It hurt my heart, hurt my soul, hurt my spirit
It still hurts the world
Allah has forsaken me
Sold my soul for his assurance of Divine protection
Futile attempts reconciling revelation with common sense
"My life and my death are all for thee..."
My truth vs. Religious loyalty
Knowing me XX chromosome non-entity

There isn't a mosque on the planet where I can hear the melody of the adhan(Muslim call to
prayer) froma female's lips
(I call the adhan)
Heretic, blasphemous, bidaa (religious innovation)
"Off with her head" would get me stoned to death
In Shariah infested "Muslim" theocracies
Ya Allah, Ya Allah
Faith shrouded in anger Give up Islam...Never
Hypocrite headed to hell
Heeding
Freak accident of DNA producing lips instead of balls...forever excluded from being
Imama (female Muslim religious leader)
Tradition, chauvinism
Inconsequential the woman's voice muzzled
An eternity of Fridays/ Jumah prayer/Seated behind the brothers/subjected to ignorant
blabbering from XY chromosome entities/Whose only qualification to preach is that he is a
MAN/Rooted in silent protest/eyes blazing/self-imposed imprisonment/fearing the 'Muslim thought police' would see my angst/Needing approval of
the community/What would Daddy think

Imagine

Me/Soldier of Allah/ 26 year old virgin/harboring secret shame/my zero sexual experience/litany
of prefixes/ Re, Su. Op-pressed/horny...but obedient/the energy consumed
by celibacy/restricting all interaction with me/no sex before marriage my mantra/ existence devoid of companionship/all touch haram (forbidden)/debates waged over
whether it was Islamically acceptable to shake a man's hand/hugging was out of the
question/ kissing...well you might as well just fornicate/ dare not talk to non-Muslim

men/while eluding sexist Muslims who expect you to be experienced
virgins who give good
head and fuck them just because they are THINKING of marrying you

Soliloquy

Obsessed every second of every hour of every day with the life and death
concern...is this
shirt long enough, are these pants too tight, does this jacket cover my ass,
do I look too
pretty, am I too attractive, have I successfully cloaked all evidence of my
sexuality...while the homiez
would laugh at me informing me they already knew how I looked under
my clothes so who
was I fooling/ Really

The Clincher

Imam W.D. Mohammed/my Imam, friend, beloved trusted mentor/like his
Daddy, Elijah, and
their penchant for pretty light skinned women young enough to be his
granddaughter/LIAR/ abusing his position and my regard/lured me to
Chicago under false
pretenses/promising an irresistible job/trying to get with me although I
was married/told me
he could make me an offer I couldn't refuse/had to ask what
the fuck can a 67 year old do for me/my foundation
shook/Betrayed/Daddy
didn't defend me/Crucified on the altar of conformity/my father chose
loyalty to
W.D./questioned everything I ever believed in/Forced to find my own
truth/My God
Nameless/Religion none/Free/Now I dwell beneath the Veil of Light
Lies they told me Lies I believed
RIP

“The emotional, sexual, and psychological stereotyping of females begins when the doctor says: "It's a girl.”

– SHIRLEY CHISHOLM

XX Experience

Used to be one of those intimidating sistas
the "Dont fuck wid me" tatted across my forehead kind
Kept my own chastity belt sealed
XX Disconnect. Sensuality disowned
Obeisance to a Man's religion
Gorgeous. 'look but don't'' touch persona.
A nice bitch
Transparent barb wire Heart defense. Pain shield
Second class inferiority, despising male species
Cloaked in casual disdain
I, Powerless, under duress
Overcompensating 'U better respect me'
Think if I weren't Muslim would probably be lesbian
Felt each unwanted pregnancy
Curse Women-manity's fucked up history
My propensity to soul forfeiting, dutiful daughter programming
Refusing to be another 'Stupid ass female'
Chip on my shoulder melded with They ancestral pleas
Anguishing every time combed hair that bore
Evidence of ancestral sexual violating
Musings of a Pissed, Potentially Murderous, Black Woman
Succumbing to hype. Seriously contemplating carrying a gun cauz
No nigga gonna rape me
Black/White world controlled by the Enemy
Feminist salvation Stoked anger flame
Each fact compiled of abuse, war, crime, hurting
Conceptualizing staging mass male lynchings for female assault
Correct the 20,000 years of sexist insanity
Could not conceive of Beingness with
Any disgustingly violent XY entity
Seeking female freedom to assuage puny victimized XX experience
Ultimate Islam induced wish. Total desexualization.

Admired for Intelligence, Righteousness
I hated, HATED being a girl Choking constriction
At the mercy of chromosomes, hormones, patriarchy
Internalizing sex oppression
Aping men Adopting masculinity Envying
Unconscious of feminine beauty energy
Past lives piling up too many memories
She-ancestors imploring. Exorcising Silenced screams
So I BREATHE pastime pain cleansing
I BREATHE connecting XX & XY humanity
I BREATHE acknowledge mutual suffering
I HEAL transmitting LightPeace radiation

"I declare to you that woman must not depend upon the protection of man, but must be taught to protect herself, and there I take my stand."

– Susan B. C Anthony

DEATH

Victimization ceased
Responsibility increased
STILL
Pathetic insecurity lingering
Envisioning reality foundering
WHILE
Excuses inflate
Lust depletes
YET
Despair increasing
Soul-life seeping
HE NICE
Prescription: Death
aka Sleeping
Until Judgment Day Screening

"Women have got to make the world safe for men since men have made it so darned unsafe for women."

– NANCY ASTOR

Psyche's Womb

Our bleeding buried, Sacred Moontime reviled
Veiled in denial. Menstrual Blood Redemption
Goddess magic Heed her sirens call
Long buried in recesses of Psyche's Womb
Memory revisited. She sits spinning arachnid dreams
Reverence the Pussy that bore you
Worshiped once again
Million droplets tears unshed A Reveal
Cleanse fear of Feminine
Mystery, Divinity AKA the Wombman

"Men are allowed to have passion and commitment for their work...a woman is allowed that feeling for a man not for her work."

– BARBARA STREISAND

MELTED

Brain Pain Freeze
Handcuffed to my silence Tongue on ice
Thoughts cubes choke in my throat
Grew a goiter Sadness spawned anger Icicles
Crystallized soulless salt

Cries deferred, iced tear-drips, blocked feelings
Chilled on lock Frosted honesty
Believing if I spoke freely he would thaw –
Leave me icy
Still abandoned Stored his neglect in my body

Stormed hurt Raging fear blizzard blanketed my world
Shivering created a cushioned distraction -thyroid disease
30 extra pounds of psychic warmth protection
My barrier to love
Dared not speak...Would die if rejected

Denied...His heat never tried to warm me
Soulthermia, Killing me coldly
My mind, the frozen cave where I dwelled. Found my sun.
Today I speak. Compelled to spit it Expression

This Zero Below *Naked Thought*
Thawed emotion released, my/our fear, shame, insecurities
Truth-sicles Ice-cream for the licking. Facilitating freedom
Voices MELTED
Speak Baby Speak

"I think women dwell quite a bit on the duress under which they work, on how hard it is just to do it all. We are traditionally rather proud of ourselves for having slipped creative work in there between the domestic chores and obligations. I'm not sure we deserve such big a-pluses for all that."

–TONI MORRISON

FULL

Womb full time No space for babies. Busy, Word gestating
Pregnant versing Birthing revolutions Nurturing sensual restoration
Phase Goddess Returns
Cradle my pussy Flooding labor pains
Bewitched pens Mid-wifing feminine reality
Clit inspired Mother-wit Unleashing
Swollen titties Drip earth wisdom
Arouse, Invigorate, Feed, Teach. Destroy like Kali
Co-Rule the world with sway of my hips. Magic milk insight
Reborn monthly in blood baptism
Womb full. Childless. Mother to the world
I am

"

"If you aren't good at loving yourself, you will have a difficult time loving anyone, since you'll resent the time and energy you give another person that you aren't even giving to yourself."

–BARBARA DE ANGELIS

UN-LOVABLE SOLILOQUY

Strong intelligent black woman, 'Stupid in love' cloaked agenda
Proving Mama wrong 'don't no man want you',
Unlovable 'too black, too ugly'
Spirit protesting!!! Maternal voice deluge, Can't hear truth
Give all. Try harder. Do more. Be nicer.
'Why can't I keep a man?'
Parental programming exorcism, Countering Daddy's
Abandonment
Casted out belief 'Don't ever trust him to stay around'
Proving Her right, Ignoring soul inklings,
'He don't treat me right'
The 'Where u been?' story,
Historic repetition, Attracted a man just like HIM
Trying to please, Digging hole deeper, He running
Desperation 'Please don't leave me'
STOP!!! Demon thoughts rattling my brain
'What she say gotta be true, Mother wouldn't lie'
I do and got everything, Still he leave me for that bitch
'Who aint got shit on me'
Don't ask for much 'Please, just convince me I'm lovable'
Madea's voice insistent
'Too much wrong wid u, aint what a man want'
Warning him 'Baby, don't get too close' 'To know me is to leave me'
Love failing never had shit to do with you,
Mommie's voice bespelled our doomed
Self-love-lack chased away, Heart wouldn't believe
You could love Unlovable me
MURDER TIME!!! Killing Dad, Silencing Mom,
Start cherishing me

"Immense power is acquired by assuring yourself in your secret reveries that you were born to control affairs."

— ANDREW CARNEGIE

Emerging

Emerging from aqueous dreams
Sea level grounding Facing vast infinities
Unshed realities, Each wave, Possibilities
Cresting, Surfing smoothly
Confidently, Wading shifting sands, Still-ly
Buoyed certainty, Awed enormity
My POWER...the Ocean ...mirroring Me

"The idea of feminine authority is so deeply embedded in the human subconscious that even after all these centuries of father-right the young child instinctively regards the mother as the supreme authority. He looks upon the father as equal with himself, equally subject to the woman's rule. Children have to be taught to love, honor, and respect the father. "

– Elizabeth Gould Davis

Sexist Apocalypse

Enter abounding love sanctuary,
Banished eternally Humanities transgressions haunted halting steps

Pain-body exorcisms, Gene memory of male subjugation by the Almighty SHE

HE's, Ashy sperm-source work drudges
Sublimated man-fear of unleashed feminine,

Released from humanities consciousness
Universal scale of female/male oppression, Balanced

Distant nightmare entering harmony's reign
Nouveau read of human history

Bastion of male privilege, Men, Black white yellow and green in agreement blinded to their suppressed recollecting

Heavens trumpets blare, Clarion call joy amplification
NOW spectre of peaceful equality

"Kundalini ...has to be awakened. Once it wakes up it starts rising upwards. When it reaches to the ultimate center of your being – SAHASRAR- the last center, the last rung of the ladder, you have arrived home"

–OSHO

KUNDALINI DREAMS

The snake lies awake in sultry reverie
Emeshed in her sinuous coil
I am evolving carnal genesis

Kundalini immersion
Sucked in her serpentine vortex
Morphed into a sex energy composition
Morphed into a sex energy composition
I Swirl...

Heart drum pulsation
Cells Strum, idea articulation, chakras hum
3rd eye flushed. Nipples juicy

An animalistic incitement
Wanna rub, fuck, mate, birth
Captured in fertilizing vibration

I Belly dance...

A psychedelic whirl.
Freedom flinging feats of arousal

Red. Green. Orange rapture
Sensual aural illumination
I climax enlightened

The snake reigns again in Kundalini Dreams

"The possibility of stepping into a higher plane is quite real for everyone. It requires no force or effort or sacrifice. It involves little more than changing our ideas about what is normal."

–Deepak Chopra

Evolving

Behind these slanted bedroom eyes lies
The content dreams are comprised
Miracles conceived in the womb of
Naked Thought perception
Subtle nuance, Intense, Mysterious, All-Seeing
Herein resides

A
former Muslim/ former Feminist/former Misogynist/former
Community Activist/
former Black Nationalist/ former 26-year old Virgin

NOW
Healer/ Sorceress/ Transformational Visionary/ Multidimensional
Light Being/ Freedom Facilitator/ Gypsy Warrior Queen
Evolving Still

NAKED THOUGHT

Poet, Word Sorcerer, Spoken Word Artist

A prolific writer *Naked Thought* has been mesmerizing audiences with performance poetry since the age of six. Multi-talented, a seeker of ultimate expression, consummate wordsmith and spoken spell weaver *Naked Thought's* poetry features multi-dimensional channeled word explorations. For *Naked Thought*, writing is an intensely personal, psychic exploration, chronicling her rapid evolution into a Being of Light. *Naked Thought* was born in Cincinnati, OH, grew up in South Central Los Angeles, moving to Texas at the age 13, where she completed high school and attended college at Prairie View A&M University. Graduating with honors from PVAMU with degrees in English and Mathematics, she relocated back to Los Angeles three years ago. A self-styled 'word ho'. *Naked Thought* impetus for her poetry is healing, transformation and evolution. Witty, cerebral, raw, and lyrical she invites all to witness the commonality of human experience. Dedicated to constantly honing and expanding her craft, for *Naked Thought* poetry is her Bliss. When *Naked Thought* isn't writing poetry, she is Academic Instructor/Tutor/Mentor for the non-profit organization, L.A.C.E.R., where she works, motivates, inspires and assists students at Fairfax High School in Los Angeles while creating and crafting her ideal reality. The author of LYRICED HONEY: The Lust Collection and FULL: a sensual evolution primer she is currently completing the other three books in her *Lyriced Honey Project*: LYRICED HONEY: Love Selections and LYRICED HONEY: Light's Refraction and LYRICED HONEY: Life Reflections and spoken word CD. *Naked Thought* recently launched her sizzling "LYRICED HONEY By NAED THOUGHT Poetry Blog" where she features her poetry, writer's workshop and other exceptional up and coming poets. Currently she is applying for the Master of Creative Writing with a Poetry concentration program at Antioch College in Los Angeles.

Contact: Naked Thought

For Booking Inquiries:

nakedthought@gmail.com 323.945.6215

www.thenakedthought.wordpress.com
www.facebook.com/NTFanPage
www.nakedthought.tumblr.com
www.thenakedthought.webs.com

NAKED BOOKS
Robertson Blvd., Beverly Hills, CA 90211

www.ingramcontent.com/pod-product-compliance
Ingram Content Group UK Ltd.
Pitfield, Milton Keynes, MK11 3LW, UK
UKHW020232250726
13967UKWH00001B/327